Māori Warriors

by Ray McClellan

BELLWETHER MEDIA · MINNEAPOLIS, MN

Are you ready to take it to the extreme?
Torque books thrust you into the action-packed world
of sports, vehicles, mystery, and adventure. These books
may include dirt, smoke, fire, and dangerous stunts.
Warning: read at your own risk.

Library of Congress Cataloging-in-Publication Data

McClellan, Ray.
 Maori warriors / by Ray McClellan.
     p. cm. -- (Torque: history's greatest warriors)
 Includes bibliographical references and index.
 Summary: "Engaging images accompany information about Maori warriors. The combination of
high-interest subject matter and light text is intended for students in grades 3 through 7"--Provided by
publisher.
 Audience: Grades 3-7.
 ISBN 978-1-60014-745-6 (hbk. : alk. paper)
 1. Maori (New Zealand people)--Warfare--Juvenile literature. 2. Maori (New Zealand people)--History--
Juvenile literature. I. Title.
 DU423.W35M43 2012
 993.01--dc23   2011028872

This edition first published in 2012 by Bellwether Media, Inc.

Printed in the United States of America, North Mankato, MN.

010112   1202

Contents

Who Were Māori Warriors?

The sounds of battle echoed through the forests of New Zealand hundreds of years ago. Tribes of Māori people fought one another for land and resources. Māori warriors were fierce and deadly. They fought in war parties called *taua*. A *taua* included between 70 and 140 warriors. A chief called a *rangatira* led the *taua*.

Battles were violent and bloody. An attacking *taua* often set up an **ambush**. They used surprise to **rout** their enemies. The winners showed no mercy. They always killed every member of the enemy *taua*. Warriors knew any survivors would seek *utu*, or revenge. The victors often ate their victims to gain their **mana**. They would also cut off their victims' heads to keep as trophies of their victory.

Māori Fact

The Māori word for "warrior" is *toa*.

Māori Warrior Training

Māori tribes needed strong warriors. Each tribe had a school of war called a *Whare Tu Taua*. This was where boys learned to become warriors. Every boy had to learn how to use weapons and protect his tribe.

Young warriors practiced using wooden spears and clubs. They learned the Māori **martial arts**. The most famous of these was *Mau Rākau*. This means "to bear a weapon."

Māori Fact

Warriors mastered the use of a long club called the *taiaha* in the martial art of *Te Mau Taiaha*.

Young warriors also perfected the *haka*. This was a dance that Māori warriors performed before battle. The *haka* featured strong and aggressive movements. It was meant to intimidate enemies.

A tribe was protected by forts called *pa*. Young warriors helped build the defenses to protect their tribe from attacks. The *pa* were surrounded by ditches, piled earth, and **palisades**. It was almost impossible for an enemy to **breach** a well-defended *pa*.

Māori Fact

Tattoos were a mark of social status and skill in battle for the Māori. One Māori could tell the importance of another by looking at his tattooed face.

Māori Warrior Equipment

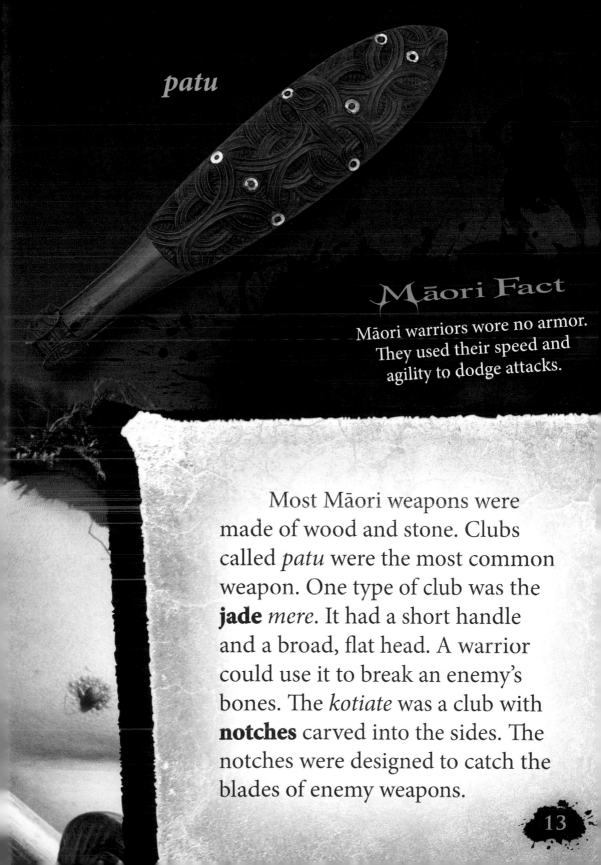

patu

Māori Fact

Māori warriors wore no armor.
They used their speed and
agility to dodge attacks.

Most Māori weapons were
made of wood and stone. Clubs
called *patu* were the most common
weapon. One type of club was the
jade *mere*. It had a short handle
and a broad, flat head. A warrior
could use it to break an enemy's
bones. The *kotiate* was a club with
notches carved into the sides. The
notches were designed to catch the
blades of enemy weapons.

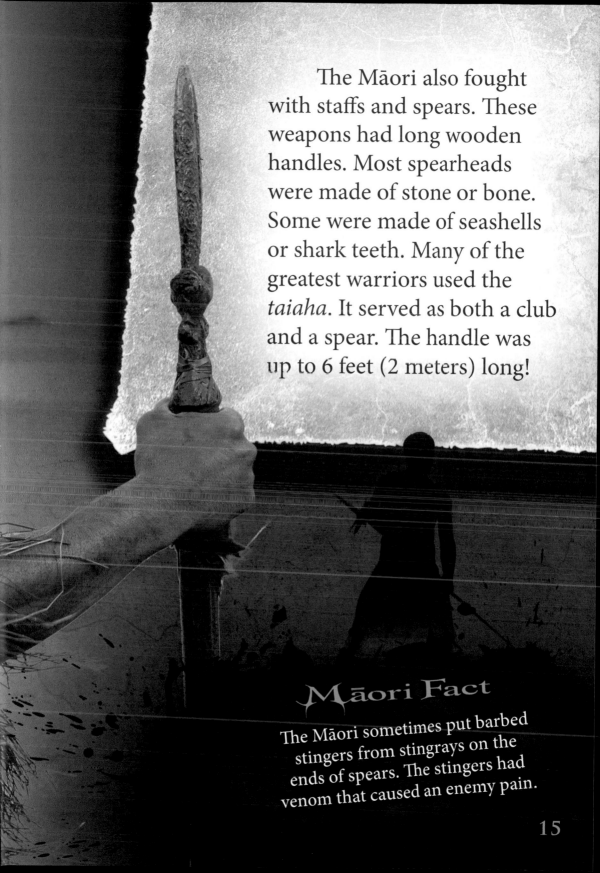

The Māori also fought with staffs and spears. These weapons had long wooden handles. Most spearheads were made of stone or bone. Some were made of seashells or shark teeth. Many of the greatest warriors used the *taiaha*. It served as both a club and a spear. The handle was up to 6 feet (2 meters) long!

Māori Fact

The Māori sometimes put barbed stingers from stingrays on the ends of spears. The stingers had venom that caused an enemy pain.

Mana

Māori warriors believed that they collected a force called mana through battle. Mana was a form of respect and spiritual power. The warriors with the most mana were a tribe's leaders.

Warriors believed they could gain a defeated enemy's mana by eating his flesh.

Defeating a powerful enemy gave a warrior more mana than defeating a weak one.

Warriors could pass their mana to their sons through their weapons.

The Decline of Māori Warriors

The Māori way of life changed when Europeans came to New Zealand. Europeans brought **muskets**. Some tribes used these guns against one another in **musket wars**. These wars were terrible and bloody. Many Māori tribes were wiped out.

Māori Fact

European explorers also carried new diseases to New Zealand. The Māori had no natural defenses against these diseases. Many of them died.

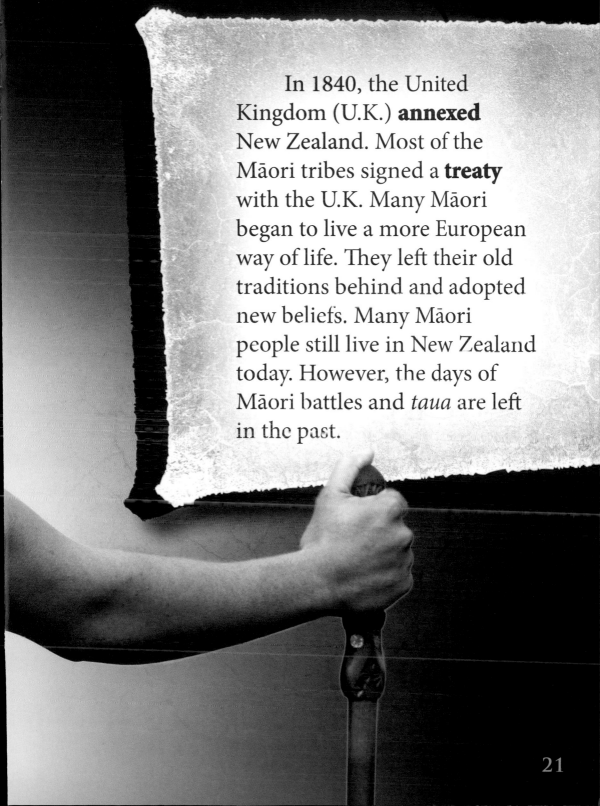

In 1840, the United Kingdom (U.K.) **annexed** New Zealand. Most of the Māori tribes signed a **treaty** with the U.K. Many Māori began to live a more European way of life. They left their old traditions behind and adopted new beliefs. Many Māori people still live in New Zealand today. However, the days of Māori battles and *taua* are left in the past.

Glossary

ambush—a sudden surprise attack from a concealed position

annexed—took ownership of a territory

breach—to break through

jade—a hard, green stone

mana—a form of respect and spiritual power earned through battle

martial arts—styles and techniques of fighting and self-defense

musket wars—intense, bloody battles fought between Māori tribes after they acquired muskets from Europeans in the first half of the 1800s

muskets—firearms that are loaded through their long barrels

notches—small indentations

palisades—walls of strong, pointed wooden stakes that stick out of the ground

rout—to defeat in a quick, overwhelming victory

treaty—a formal agreement between two or more groups

To Learn More

AT THE LIBRARY

Graham, Pita. *Maori Legends of the Land: Maori Tales and Traditions*. Takapuna, N.Z.: Bush Press of New Zealand, 2002.

Strudwick, Leslie. *Maori*. New York, N.Y.: Weigl Publishers, 2005.

Theunissen, Steve. *The Maori of New Zealand*. Minneapolis, Minn.: Lerner Publications Co., 2003.

ON THE WEB

Learning more about Māori warriors is as easy as 1, 2, 3.

1. Go to www.factsurfer.com.

2. Enter "Maori warriors" into the search box.

3. Click the "Surf" button and you will see a list of related Web sites.

With factsurfer.com, finding more information is just a click away.

Index